Flying High:
Life lessons from the Big Top

Flying High: Life lessons from the Big Top

SHELLI EPSTEIN

StoryTerrace

Several of the names in this book have been changed for privacy of individuals.

Text Shelli Epstein and Mark Ledsom, on behalf of StoryTerrace

Design StoryTerrace

Copyright © Shelli Epstein

Second print January 2023

StoryTerrace

www.StoryTerrace.com

CONTENTS

PROLOGUE	7
CHAPTER 1	9
CHAPTER 2	17
CHAPTER 3	23
CHAPTER 4	33
CHAPTER 5	41
CHAPTER 6	49
CHAPTER 7	57
CHAPTER 8	65
CHAPTER 9	75
CHAPTER 10	87
CHAPTER 11	101
CHAPTER 12	111
CHAPTER 13	117
CHAPTER 14	127
EPILOGUE	137

"Dreams do come true, if only we wish hard enough."
                                     J.M. Barrie, Peter Pan

PROLOGUE

"So many of our dreams at first seem impossible, then they seem improbable, and then, when we summon the will, they soon become inevitable."

Christopher Reeve

Running away to join the circus has become a cliché for the sort of childhood dreams that so many of us harbour until the point that we 'grow up' and shift our attention to 'adult responsibilities'. I have the utmost respect for all forms of accomplishment and realise that many people are fulfilled by achieving mastery in their chosen professions but, when I see crowds of suited workers heading into and out of their offices every day, I do sometimes wonder how many of them are truly passionate about what they do, or whether they have compromised on their dreams of becoming an astronaut, racing car driver or musician.

At the age of 11, I told my parents that I wanted to join the circus. We had just been to see the world's most successful circus company, Cirque du Soleil, performing at London's Royal Albert Hall and I had been mesmerised. I remember being enthralled by the characters, the movement, the music and the production. There were people walking on giant balls, jumping through hoops and gliding on silks – which are large fabrics where the acrobats twist, turn and drop, leaving the audience with their jaws hanging open. Overall, though, I just remember being in awe of it all – seeing people flying through the air and thinking, *I'd love to do that.*

All too often, people abandon their childhood dreams because they believe (or are made to believe) that they are too fanciful, too ludicrous, impossible even. If there is one thing I want people to take away from my story, it's that almost any dream can be realised – if it is what you truly want and are prepared to work hard for it.

So what happened to that 11-year-old girl sat in the plush red seats, staring up in awe at her first circus? Well, without giving away too much, she came back to the Royal Albert Hall 16 years later when Cirque du Soleil returned to present their latest show, *Luzia*. This time, however, she didn't need a ticket as she was now one of those people flying high above the stage.

I did indeed join the circus. This is the story of how I did it, and it is dedicated to the dreamers.

1

"It's kind of fun to do the impossible."

Walt Disney

When people ask me about my family background, they often seem to think that circus performers are born into circus families. That may have been the case in the past, and still is today in certain parts of the world. When it comes to modern, international circus companies, though, my experience has been that most of the performers come from 'regular' families and are usually the only member of their family to have gone into the circus profession. That was certainly the case with me. I was born in Israel but moved to the UK before my first birthday, and grew up as the eldest of three children in a conventional north London family.

I was a tumbler long before I could talk. By the time I was six months old, my mother didn't know what to do with me as I was so hyperactive. To get rid of my excess energy, she took me to the baby gym for double sessions. At that stage, we lived on the fourth floor of an apartment block with sash windows that had to be nailed down at all times, as I would make a beeline for them.

By the time I was four, I had been selected for my local gymnastics squad. Although I was still very young, my mother has since reminded me that I was utterly useless on the selection day – not flexible, not listening to instructions. What I did have going for me, however, was enthusiasm and a love for the gym, and that's what the selectors saw. It was a lesson that has served me many times since: if you are truly passionate about something you love, it will radiate and shine right through you.

My passion for gymnastics stayed with me for another eight years and consumed virtually all my spare time – or rather, the time that would have been spare if I hadn't been using it to train, and to travel back and forth from training. My parents were incredible in the support they gave me: working hard to provide for my training, sacrificing their time to drive me all over the country for events and competitions and (most importantly) supporting me emotionally and without pressure. My mum always told me that I could quit whenever I wanted. They were never pushy parents.

When I was seven, we moved back to Israel (for my dad's

work) for a couple of years, and I auditioned for Hapoel Tel Aviv gymnastics club. Starting school in a foreign country was tough, particularly learning a new language. All the lessons, apart from English, were taught in Hebrew, so I missed out on a lot of information during those years. But at least my gymnastics continued without any major disruption as my coaches were from Romania and were fluent in English as well as Hebrew.

They had a stereotypically Eastern European attitude when it came to discipline and performance, which even extended to my social life outside gymnastics. Once, when I was invited to a birthday party, my coach gave my mother an earful: "Shelli is either 100% committed or she's not." There was no middle ground for a seven-year-old who wished to go to birthday parties!

My grandparents live in Israel, and it was wonderful to have my grandfather collect me at the end of my gym sessions on his way home from work. On reflection, that was a special time for me as I never again had the luxury of living close to my grandparents after those two years spent in Israel.

After returning to the UK at the age of 10, I briefly rejoined my previous gymnastics club in Hendon. One of my coaches, who was about to leave for another club, secured us an audition at Heathrow Gymnastics Club, which is a national-level club. In the end, four of us got places at the club, which helped a lot with lift-sharing as Heathrow was a long drive, especially in rush-hour traffic.

This was the stage when gymnastics became really serious. Although we were barely into double digits, all of the top gymnasts were already starting to think about competing at the Olympics – and the intensity heightened when London was selected to host the 2012 Games. By the time the Games took place, we would all be in our late teens and at our peak as gymnasts.

This was the first time in my life that I began to wrestle with the idea of the possible and the impossible. Some gymnasts were staying at a boarding school close to the gym so that they could dedicate their lives fully to gymnastics before and after school. I slowly started to question whether I was committed enough to gain a place at the Olympics.

As my doubts increased, my love for the sport began to fade. There were days when I would cry and just hate it: days where I was no longer doing gymnastics out of joy and love for the sport. Gymnastics is a highly individual and competitive sport, and I began to feel that the probability of me realising my Olympic dream was very low. After looking around at other opportunities and after much deliberation, I decided to leave Heathrow and I joined a team gym called Childs Hill Gymnastics Display Team, where they practised display gymnastics.

On reflection, I learned two lessons, and they kind of contradict each other. But that's ok. Life lessons don't usually come in black and white!

> **LIFE LESSON #1: It's far too easy to believe that things are far too difficult.**

I made the mistake of comparing myself to the gymnasts around me and what they were achieving rather than believing more in myself and focusing on what I was capable of.

> **LIFE LESSON #2: If you really want to succeed at something then you have to have a passion for it. If the flame in your heart dims, then your desire to strive for your goal also fades.**

The spark reignited when I abandoned the Olympic dream and stepped into something new. Sometimes we need to pause, take a break, and embrace something new. I gave up on my Olympic dream and another door opened. I was now part of a team as opposed to being an individual. I couldn't have imagined at that time, however, that this opportunity would eventually take me to the big top and fulfil another dream.

Little Shelli

Little Shelli

Little Shelli as a gymnast at Hapoel Tel Aviv in Israel

2

"Schools always appeared to me like a prison, and never could I make up my mind to stay there, not even for four hours a day, when the sunshine was inviting, the sea smooth, and when it was joy to run about the cliffs in the free air, or to paddle in the water."

Claude Monet

I had said goodbye to my Olympic dream but had embarked on a new journey with my display gymnastics team. Display gymnastics includes tumbling and acrobatics, and there are also elements of dance and performing. I hadn't even known that this genre of gymnastics existed, but it instantly reminded me of the Cirque du Soleil show that I'd seen at the Royal Albert Hall not long before, and it just looked so much fun.

At my very first session, I fell in love with the sport. I loved being thrown around, but I also made lots of friends, and it really taught me how to be part of a team. From the age of 12 to 18, we took part at gymnastics festivals up and down the country, and even represented the UK at international events.

Childs Hill morphed me into the performer that I am today and taught me how to hold a stage and audience. I remember them telling me that if you can see the audience, they can see you. They also taught me that the heaviest part of your body is your eyes, because if you look down, then you will go down. In a biology lesson at school, we were asked if anybody knew what the heaviest part of the body was. I repeated what I'd learned at Childs Hill and everybody laughed. The biology teacher had meant the question literally. It still makes me smile when I think about that. My coaches recognised my potential and helped me to develop the discipline's performance side in particular. Years later, I was able to invite one of my coaches to see me perform for Cirque, and we laughed as we reminisced about how shy I had been at first, and how I had never wanted to be in the spotlight.

I applied to a senior school that specialised in dance. I had to audition for a place, and passed. The entry requirements made it mandatory to take lunch-time and after-school dance classes, alongside my academic obligations. I learned and enjoyed contemporary dance, which complemented my new gymnastics style of movements.

I was fortunate enough to have a fantastic and inspirational PE teacher, Ros van Oostrum, who took a keen interest in my abilities and encouraged me to join the trampolining team. The school took trampolining seriously, and I started learning how to jump and use the equipment properly. I began going to school early, before the classrooms opened, just to train. It was at that time that the Olympic torch flickered briefly for me, once again, as the teacher in charge of trampolining put my name forward (without my knowledge) as a candidate for the potential 2012 Olympics GB diving team.

I went to the audition and was selected for the team! Training would take place at the Crystal Palace Diving Centre which was a huge commitment as it was a three- to four-hour commute there and back, and was mainly 'dry', i.e. in the training facilities rather than the pool. This involved working with harnesses and trampolines and doing lots of drills and conditioning. It all came to a sudden end, however, when they discovered asbestos at the diving centre and had to close the pool down for a major refurbishment. The diving team operations were relocated to Leicester, which was *way* too far, thus my Olympic dream was terminated.

In year 10, I was offered a place at another school that my sister was already attending. In order for my place to be confirmed, I had to first pass an interview. As I was only

14 at the time, my mum also had to be in the room. One of the questions they asked was about what I wanted to do when I eventually left school. When I replied that I wanted to be a circus performer or maybe a stunt double, I saw my mum's head literally drop into her hands, as she assumed I had blown the interview. In fact, the interviewer seemed impressed and simply said, "That's refreshing!" Anyway, I got the place.

I soon found myself chugging along on the academic treadmill. The school pushed me hard academically and helped me get good results in my GCSEs. But my experiences there also reinforced my view that, at the end of the day, grades are not everything. We put so much pressure on children from such a young age to do well in exams, and make them believe that academic success is all that matters in shaping their future. In the real world outside of school there are many possibilities beyond the 'normal' options. And I feel that you cannot generalise regarding people's future pathways. We are all different and thrive at different activities, professions and elements. In my opinion schools should nurture young people to excel in the things that they are good at, help them to improve and steer them in the direction that best suits their interests and abilities.

I achieved the grades I required – better grades than I'd even thought possible – but I struggled to fit in socially. I did have a couple of close friends, but I also remember days when I would eat my lunch in the changing rooms just to be away from everybody. School is definitely a challenging place, particularly in your teens when you have all this pressure from your parents and teachers and all these crazy hormones racing through your system that you are trying to learn to control. I felt like an adult but, looking back now, I realise I wasn't. I was still learning. You always are.

After GCSEs, the treadmill continued on to A-levels. I wanted to take dance as one of my subjects but my school didn't offer it. They did, however, let me find another school (the Royal Academy of Dance) where I could take the course on Saturdays. This involved three hours of theory and three hours of practical – so took up pretty much the whole Saturday and meant missing out on a lot of social events. This wasn't anything new to me after all those years on the road with my gymnastics clubs, so I didn't really mind, and I got to make new friends at the academy, who had similar interests to my own.

By the time I turned 18, I was set for my final year of school and feeling all the same pressures as my contemporaries, i.e. to follow the same road, to complete our A-levels and to apply for university places. I looked into a few university courses but really had no idea what I wanted to study. There were courses related to sport and exercise sciences which appealed to me, but I had no real understanding of what they entailed, until I visited the universities and realised that they were research based. After receiving a low grade in biology, I had to pause and take a fresh look at what I really wanted to do. I was encouraged to follow my heart and do what I truly wanted, which was circus/dance, and began exploring those avenues instead. I started to look at arts courses including dance and even circus arts – which you can now study at a couple of places in the UK as a full Bachelor of Arts degree. That was a real 'Aha!' moment for me.

> **LIFE LESSON #3: Sometimes in life, you have to step off the treadmill to find the real opportunities.**

That was certainly the case with my own story. I did find my way into circus, but not via university. In fact, in true carnival style, I was drawn to the big top after seeing a poster…

3

"If somebody offers you an amazing opportunity but you are not sure you can do it, say yes – then learn how to do it later."
   Richard Branson

I continued to train at Childs Hill, but also sometimes went to Hendon to take some adult gym classes. Hendon had a sprung floor and a foam pit, so I could play around and try out some things that I couldn't do at Childs Hill, where we only had mats on wooden floors.

It was while I was at Hendon one day that I saw the poster that would change my life. It was advertising an audition that would be taking place in London for the Franco Dragone entertainment group and their new show, *The House of Dancing Water*. I was a huge fan of Franco Dragone, who had been influential in the development of Cirque du Soleil and many of the company's most successful productions before heading off to set up his own company in 2000. Just the thought of being able to audition for one of his spectacular shows was enough to send shivers down my spine. It was more a case of wanting to check out the audition process and see what level of skills I would need if I ever wanted to make it into a professional circus one day.

The day that I chose to bunk off school to get to the audition didn't really go to plan. Traffic wasn't kind and there were delays and closures on various routes on the underground. I'm usually a very organised person, but on the day that I needed to make a good impression, everything seemed to be working against me.

> **LIFE LESSON #4: First impressions are everything. Never be late for an audition.**

I arrived late.

By the time I got there, everyone else had been given their audition numbers and had been able to warm up. They could have turned me away, however I was fortunate that the audition was being organised by a wonderful guy called Joseph. He would later become both my mentor and a good friend but, for now, he was just a sympathetic stranger telling me to relax and he assured me that I could still audition.

He did me a huge favour, but it didn't always feel that way over the course of the next few hours as my fellow auditionees and I were put through some of the most gruelling tests I have ever experienced. The first round was tumbling, and they asked us to demonstrate a forward pass, backward pass, side pass and something "that makes you stand out". For this, I just put some random skills together. Since I hadn't warmed up, I could already feel pain as the blood rushed into my stiff wrists and ankles. Once we'd finished, they were randomly calling out numbers. You didn't know if you wanted your number to be called out or not. I was hoping mine would be, thinking it would be positive. However, the outcome of the numbers that were called from that round, were then sent home. Luckily, my number was not called.

Next up was conditioning. I must have been pumped with adrenaline, because I managed some moves and skills that I haven't been able to replicate since! This, honestly, was one of the hardest tests of fitness I have ever experienced, and it amazes me to this day when I consider what the human body is capable of and what it can endure.

After the conditioning, there was another cut, and we moved onto trampolining into a foam pit. My training at Hendon helped me out here, as I was able to throw a double front, which I'd only pulled off a couple of times previously.

Then came a test of our flexibility, which was still a weak point for me. I solemnly thought that it would be the end for me, but somehow I succeeded in getting through. Maybe I was especially limbered up from the conditioning work or perhaps it was the adrenaline. Either way, I made the cut.

All day long, they threw challenges at us and, all day long, they kept reading out the numbers of the people they were sending home. Finally, we got to the dancing test, which was all about seeing how quickly we could pick up choreography. We were given a piece that I would later learn to know as the 'war' sequence from one of the acts in the show, and made to perform it after a rapid run-through of the moves. This was one part of the day where I felt at an advantage, thanks to my dance school experience.

When it was all over, they split us into two groups – this time calling out our names rather than our numbers, so that we had no idea which group was the one being sent home. Luckily, I was in the right group. Once the others had left, they gathered us all together and said, "Congratulations, you've made it past day one," and in my head, I was like, *Day one? Does that mean there's a day two?!*

There was indeed, and I was even more confused when they told us that we would be meeting the next day at a nearby swimming pool. I had done no research whatsoever into the show that I was auditioning for and had no idea why swimming was relevant. I remembered that the show did have 'dancing water' in the title, but I didn't dare ask anyone. Feeling absolutely shattered (but also elated), I headed home and finally told my parents all about my crazy day. I tried to prepare myself for more of the same in the morning.

For the second day of the audition, I drove straight to the pool – not wanting to take the risk of public transport again. My body ached from the previous day and I wasn't sure I had the endurance for another day of physical strain. It made me think about the life I was potentially choosing for myself and wonder how these superhuman performers manage to keep going day in, day out.

We started with a pretty demanding test of our basic swimming ability that included speed laps, laps holding our breath, push-ups out of the water onto the (very high) pool edge and timed periods of treading water, before moving over to the diving pool, where they really started to have fun with us. They instructed us to 'dolphin dive' and then gave critical feedback, I somehow felt it was more of a test of seeing if we were comfortable hitting the water at an awkward angle. We then moved on to front and back 'cavemans', which was something new and fun for me. A caveman is basically a jump where you enter the water folded in half. For a front caveman, you enter the water with your hands, feet and head tucked inwards, whereas for a backwards caveman you enter the water butt-first, holding onto your hands and feet.

Finally, it was time for the five-metre diving tower. Here,

I think, they were looking to see how we coped with fear, as five metres can feel like quite a way up if you haven't done much diving before. In my head, I was telling myself that I had to demonstrate I could do something outside of my comfort zone, something that scared me. I also reasoned that they wouldn't make us do anything that might actually hurt us (although, afterwards, I remembered that we all had to sign a waiver freeing the company from any liability if we did get injured!). So, I literally threw myself into it and did everything that was demanded. By the time we were told to dry off and get changed, I felt pretty chuffed with myself.

There were no cuts being made on that second day. This marked the end of the physical section of the audition process with a short interview to wrap it all up. The interview turned out to be the cringiest experience of my life! My total lack of pre-audition research catching me off guard.

One of the things they were particularly keen to hear was why I wanted to be in a Franco Dragone show. I panicked and started jabbering on about my love of Cirque du Soleil (where Franco had started his journey. Cirque was now his company's main rival) and telling them what a fan I was of 'Guy Lambert'. I was talking about Guy (pronounced 'Ghee') Laliberté, the inspirational founder of Cirque, who had gone from being a humble street performer to almost single-handedly reinventing circus and creating a world-class enterprise that would dominate its field for decades.

Unfortunately, I had only read about him and had never heard his name said out loud, so I just blurted out 'Guy Lambert'. I'm sure they had no idea why I was going on so much about their main rivals, or who the hell this Guy Lambert character was, hopefully they had a good laugh about it once I'd gone. To make things worse, the interview was filmed. That's one recording I never want to see again!

> **LIFE LESSON #5:** Cirque du Soleil was *not* founded by Guy Lambert!

Before leaving the audition, we were told that the company would be in touch with us in January, they also explained that being selected was not only a matter of how well we had performed over the previous two days. The way that circus casting works is that when an artist leaves a show, the casting team need to replace him or her with someone of a similar profile. This was all new language to me, and I tried my utmost to follow everything I was being told.

Once January came along, I had it in my head that I would hear on a specific date. When that date came and went and I still didn't hear anything for another two weeks, I figured that I hadn't been chosen. It was too good to be true, I thought, and told myself to be grateful for the experience.

Then, one evening, everything changed. I was sitting

at home watching a football game on TV for some reason. Seriously, I *never* watch football. And this meant that I was in the one part of the house where there is no phone signal. So, rather than getting a call, I got an email asking me to call the Franco Dragone people. My fingers trembled as I pressed in the numbers.

Joseph took the call but I can barely remember the details of what he said other than the main detail of me being offered the job! At this point, I mentioned that I was still in school and had my exams to sit in May but Joseph told me not to worry, that we would figure it all out, and there was still plenty of time before I needed to head to Macau.

Ah yes, Macau! That was one of the other details to which I hadn't paid too much attention! The new show was going to be staged in Macau, but I wasn't exactly sure where that was. Somewhere close to Hong Kong? After thanking the Franco Dragone people for their faith in me and telling them how much I was looking forward to starting my training, I hung up and quickly checked out Google Maps.

I then ran to find my parents and, with a huge grin on my face, blurted out, "Mum, dad, I'm moving to China!"

Macau, New Year's Eve 2014, world's tallest bungee (233m)

4

"In university, we are taught a lesson then given a test. Whereas in life, we are given a test that teaches us a lesson."

Habeeb Akande

My parents' reaction to the news was incredulous, nothing that I had expected. I had expected them to try and talk me out of this crazy unconventional commitment. However, they were totally chilled with the idea and didn't question my decision. They completely supported it. Strangely I don't remember questioning myself. I can be equally prone to self-doubt as the next person, but when it came to joining Franco Dragone I instinctively knew that this is what I wanted, so I never paused to think about the consequences or the challenges involved in leaving my family behind and flying off to a foreign land. The morning after receiving the phone call, I made a call of my own – to withdraw my university applications.

It wasn't a straightforward case of being selected at the audition and flying directly to Macau. First, I would have to undergo three months of training in Franco Dragone's home country, Belgium. On 21st May 2012, my dad drove me to St Pancras train station, where I was due to board the Eurostar train for Brussels, and simply let me out by the main entrance before driving off again. There weren't any parking spaces for him to pull into and I was already running a bit late owing to the London traffic (again), so I understand why he couldn't see me onto the train. Still, it felt like a bit of a low-key 'goodbye' as I headed off to start my big adventure.

The station was absolutely heaving and I felt a rising sense of panic as I desperately pushed my way towards the departure board to find out which platform the train was leaving from. Fortunately, I bumped into one of the other girls who I had met at the audition, Lilly, who was also looking rather flustered and, together, we managed to pick out our platform and make it past security and through the ticket gates just in time to make it on board. We checked the tickets that the company had sent us and made our way to the designated carriage where we found another of the successful auditionees, Julia, waiting for us. After stowing our luggage and settling in for the journey, we joked about how much it reminded us of the first *Harry Potter* film, as the first years headed off to wizard school on the Hogwarts Express.

From Brussels, we continued our journey by local train until we reached Kontich – the small, sleepy town in the north of Belgium that was to be our home for the next three months. We lived in our training facility, which looked more like a warehouse and was divided into different sections. There was the dry training space, the swimming pool and diving tower, the studio for workshops, an outside lounge area, kitchen and dining space. Then, upstairs, the accommodation. This was arranged as apartments, each of which had two bedrooms and bathrooms as well as a small living area and kitchen. It didn't look anything like Hogwarts, but it did have a sense of arriving somewhere magical. All the people were exactly like me, and understood me, I finally felt that I belonged.

But while the people around me were great, my time in Belgium was tough. I had never experienced anything like it. It was three months of vigorous training. Three months of learning the entire show. Every weekday, we would wake up, train, have a lunch break (during which I'd also squeeze in some studying), train and then go to bed. Training would consist of a warm-up followed by conditioning and then a mix of different exercises from dance, improv and movement classes to partner-work, show-related disciplines and (once we'd built enough of a repertoire) training on the actual apparatus. There was also swimming, diving and scuba-diving training. I was fully aware by now that water formed a big part of the show!

I had very little 'down time', as I was still doing my A-levels in psychology, PE and dance. When we found out that I would be moving to Belgium, we managed to transfer my examinations to a school in Antwerp which offered the same exam boards as the UK. Every Saturday, while the rest of the group headed out on day trips or just to explore the local area, I would be stuck in my room studying. Some days, I had to miss training to sit my exams. One of the trainers was not particularly sympathetic towards me and would call me out in front of everyone. "See, you don't know the choreography, because you weren't here!" I would just nod and try harder, and then go to my room and cry afterwards, because I didn't want to break down in front of her.

It was hard and it was intense, but I loved every minute of it. Our trainers would replicate as much of the show as possible. We could watch videos sent over from Macau and recreate the performance in the much smaller confines of our training facility. My body was often covered in bruises, either from misjudged water entries or the harness or the chandelier apparatus. I tried to make a bruise log-diary when my legs were black and blue – they always looked worse than they actually were!

One huge disappointment was the fact that all this was happening simultaneously with the London 2012 Olympics. Competing at those Games had been such an ambition for much of my younger life that it felt heart-breaking not to even be in London and experience the buzz that filled the city during that fantastic fortnight. Instead, I was cloistered away in a nondescript corner of Belgium and only managed to catch a few of the highlights on TV.

After what seemed a lifetime, the end of our training in Belgium began to draw to a close. I had also taken my final A-level exams. When the company announced that they would be throwing us all a big social barbecue, it felt like I could finally let my hair down. I had no idea that this barbecue would, in fact, provide me with the sternest (and nastiest) challenge of the entire three months…

> **LIFE LESSON #6:** Don't let your professional guard down in a work setting - even if (or especially if) it's disguised as a social event.

As we all enjoyed the warm summer evening over plates of hot food and glasses of chilled wine, I started chatting with one of the people in the management team. He asked me what I thought was a harmless enough question about my thoughts on the imminent move out to Macau. Perhaps I was naive, but I answered honestly, telling him that I was a little scared at the idea of living so far away from home and that I'd feel anxious about getting a flat on my own anywhere, let alone in China.

I still think those are perfectly reasonable anxieties for an 18-year-old who is about to upend her life and move to the other side of the world, but he took my words and used them against me. I hadn't realised it when we first went to Belgium, but there were two people in our group who only had short-term contracts with the company, unlike the rest of us who had full two-year contracts, and I am convinced that they wanted to transfer my contract to one of the girls who was on a temporary arrangement.

Two weeks before we were due to leave for Macau, I was called into the office for a meeting, where they told me that I was too young to be given a two-year contract. They said that they would be giving my contract to the other girl instead, but that I could still come to Macau for three months. After that, I would return home and they would call me if and when they needed me.

To say I was shocked would be an understatement. I was 18. The other girl had only just turned 19. And they had known how old I was when they hired me.

It hurt, but instead of feeling helpless or sorry for myself, I used it to fuel my determination and desire. I told myself that I wasn't going to go through all this for nothing. I was going to fulfil my dream. I was going to work harder. For the last two weeks in Belgium, I did just that. I really pushed myself and started to do the bigger tricks that scared me. I did them regardless. I was going to prove that I deserved my place.

Belgium, 2012, scuba diving training in the pool for one of the cues on the show

5

"The real act of discovery consists not in finding new lands but in seeing with new eyes."

Marcel Proust

If Belgium felt like a different world compared to my life back home in London, Macau was another universe! I was prepared for the heat, but I remember being literally ambushed by the humidity, not to mention the sounds, sights and smells.

We had finished up in Kontich and been given a few days to go home and see our families, before meeting up again at Heathrow for the long flight east. After landing in Doha, we transferred to Hong Kong and then headed straight to the ferry port that is located within the airport. Having not actually seen anything of Doha or Hong Kong, my first real sense of being in Asia only came when I stepped onto the ferry, feeling that hot, damp air soaking into my skin and my clothes, and grimacing at the overpowering scent of my fellow passengers' steaming noodle bowls.

After an hour's ride across some pretty choppy waters, we disembarked at the bustling Macau ferry terminal and got a glimpse of our new home. It was like nowhere I had ever been before: a bewildering melting pot of old Portuguese colonial-era buildings mixed in with scruffy-looking Chinese shops and residential blocks, and topped off by a huddle of modern skyscrapers, shopping malls and big, glitzy casinos that looked as if they'd been airlifted in from Las Vegas. It felt like Vegas on steroids.

Our first port of residence was a pretty dated hotel in the centre of town. The breakfasts in that place were also a sight to behold; with so many guests from all over the world to cater to, they would prepare these staggering buffets with just about everything you could imagine (and some things you'd never imagine) from noodles and soups to unspecified meats and all sorts of unidentified floating objects. I stuck to toast and jam.

Walking the streets around the hotel, I got the impression that it wasn't the cleanest of places – and I never got used to the locals' constant burping and spitting – but it certainly wasn't filthy either. Macau's Portuguese past helped lend it a certain old-world charm, and the people were generally friendly and helpful. In fact, the only local residents I never particularly took to were Macau's giant flying cockroaches!

The main spoken languages were Portuguese and Cantonese but, apart from some basic words of Cantonese for dealing with taxi drivers, I didn't learn either. For work, English was the language used by the company, so I was lucky in that sense.

In many ways, the situation with the languages encapsulates the bubble that we were living in during that time in Macau. All around us was this noisy, colourful, Chinese city and there we were, a bunch of English-speaking international circus artists and technical support staff, ensconced (during our working hours at least) in the closed-off world of our show.

There are three main types of show when it comes to major international circuses. There are resident shows, where the show is set up permanently (or at least, for years) in one location – usually a place visited by lots of tourists. The Las Vegas shows are perhaps the most famous example of these. Cirque du Soleil's longest-running show, *Mystère*, has been running in Las Vegas for nearly 30 years and *The House of Dancing Water* in Macau was also a resident show, staged in a theatre that was purpose-built for the show. Residences have the advantage that you can really build a life for yourself in the location. In fact, I have some friends who have been in Macau from when the show started, more than 10 years ago.

At the other end of the scale (when it comes to how much

time you spend in a location) are the arena shows, where you move to a new city almost every week. You set up, train, perform and then tear the whole set down again, ready to move on to the next town. I've never done an arena show and, to be honest, I'm not sure I could. Living out of a suitcase, never having time to explore the place you're in – I don't think it would be for me.

Then, in between the residences and the arenas, there are the big top shows, where you set up in a location for weeks, sometimes months, and are usually put up in an apartment that you can turn into a temporary home, rather than being stuck in a hotel room. That was the type of show I moved onto when I later joined Cirque du Soleil, and I'd say it's definitely my favourite type, as it gives you the chance not only to travel, but also to really get to know the places that you're visiting.

There are also differences when it comes to the people working on the different types of production. For arena shows and big tops, you have a core group of performers who travel to all of the locations but these are then supplemented by local 'fly-ins' who might join the show for a particular leg, such as the European or US sections. Those type of shows also tend to rely on local technicians for helping with the set-up and tear-down as well as employing local staff in the box office, for front-of-house roles and as ushers. In Macau, as a residence show, we were one fixed group – from the technicians and the ushers to the performers and managers.

That gives you more of a sense of being one big family, but it can also make it harder to build a life for yourself away from the all-encompassing world of the show.

And what a show *The House of Dancing Water* was! On our first full day in Macau, we were given the chance to sit through a whole performance. My only regret was that I kept checking my phone as it was the day that everyone at my old school in London was getting their exam results and I didn't want to miss out on all the news. I wish I had just switched it off, though, as there is nothing like watching a show in the flesh for the first time. We had obviously seen the different scenes in training but watching it on a laptop screen hardly compares to seeing it for real, particularly when it's a show on the scale of *The House of Dancing Water*.

The show was housed in its own purpose-built $250-million theatre and includes a hydraulic stage that rises out of – and then sinks back into – a 3.7-million-gallon swimming pool (more than five times the volume of an Olympic pool). This is deep enough for the performers to dive into from heights of up to 25 metres – two-and-a-half times the height of the tallest Olympic diving board. And to think, I'd been wondering during my London audition why on earth we needed to meet at a swimming pool!

To further enhance the magic of the show, Franco Dragone had come up with a system that allowed the artists to splash into the water and never re-emerge (for example, when portraying a pirate who has fallen from the rigging of his ship during a storm, never to be seen again). Without giving too many of the show's secrets away, this was achieved using a series of underwater escape tunnels and a team of 30 scuba divers (sometimes disguised as sharks with their dorsal fins sticking out of the water) who would be at hand to give us oxygen under water.

My parents once came out to see the show and were able to sit in one of the technical booths. This is really interesting as one can experience the entire production being 'called' by the director. This includes the action on the stage, but also behind the scenes, as the scuba divers, lighting engineers and special effects team are all given their instructions. It is a whole other show besides the one you see on stage – an incredible coming together of spectacular artistry and ingenious technical flair.

Anyway, I'd finally got to see the show for myself. Now there was just the small matter of becoming part of it!

The House Of Dancing Water - Chandelier

6

"Our greatest glory is not in never failing, but in rising every time we fall."

Confucius

The next three months of settling in were fast-paced and, at times, overwhelming. We were worked hard, with lots of training sessions, costume fittings, and scuba lessons – not only did we have to master the equipment, but we also had to learn the different paths and tracks under the water. However, I soon got used to navigating my way around the underwater sections of the set. It was like a maze at first but, once you figured it out, it became like home, albeit a very strange, underwater home!

The show was divided into six main acts ('Boat', 'Chandelier', 'Pagoda', 'Straps', 'Russian swing' and 'War') and six cues. Cues are when you are not taking part in your main act but are on stage as an accessory or to help other performers in their act.

The show opens with a typical Chinese fishing boat that gets caught in a storm. The fisherman-hero later emerges on a huge pirate ship on one of three golden masts (with gold representing good luck in China). This was my favourite scene of the show, as the pirates reawaken from being stuck underwater for years. Slowly, we would emerge from the water after hearing our cue: "Performers five, six, seven, eight, up, up, up."

As the lightning flashes all around, the performers scale the rigging and swing from mast to mast, or else lose their footing in the turmoil and tumble to their watery 'deaths'. I remembered being terrified back in Belgium on the first day of training for this sequence, when we'd been asked to leap from the lowest height (a 'mere' nine metres), but I managed to do it and was soon building somersaults and other tricks into my routine, so was pretty much able to pick up where I'd left off when it came to jumping off the real apparatus in Macau.

After the boat scene, there was just enough time to dry off and change before the chandelier act. This involved performing tricks as one of eight couples dangling five meters above the swimming pool from a huge birdcage-like structure that descends into position from the roof of the theatre. According to the story, we were slave entertainers performing for the pleasure of the dark queen. Had anyone fallen during this performance, the sharks (scuba divers) would swoop in on them, leaving the audience believing that they had been devoured. Great fun for the spectators, but falling into the water was certainly not something you'd want to do, especially from a handstand position five metres above the pool. The problem was that our hands were often still wet from our previous scene and it was also easy to slip off if our wet costumes came into contact with the chandelier's foam padding.

The Russian swing is a traditional circus act that usually involves acrobats leaping from a swinging platform onto a mat or, in its scariest version, onto another swinging platform. I'd always sworn to myself that I would *never* do the swing-to-swing version. It is extremely dangerous and carries huge risk – we will check in with that promise later in my story! In Macau, though, I 'only' had to fly from the swing into the water. We were acting as minions of the dark queen, preparing for war or just messing around and showing off, and it was a lot of fun. Still, you needed to have your wits about you as we had four swings operating at the same time and had to make sure that we didn't land on the person who had just left the other swing. We had something like 13 scuba divers working on that part of the show and giving us the signals that it was safe to jump. The finale was the scariest part as we had to perform a blind jump into the water and then grab hold of an underwater regulator (painted bright yellow to help us find it) so that we could breathe, put on a mask and make our way back to the 'beach' area.

Those first three months of integrating into the show were exhausting and exhilarating in equal measure, but I gave it everything I had. After two weeks, I was called into the office for a meeting with the management team, which felt ominously similar to being summoned in Belgium two weeks prior to the end of training and having my full-time contract revoked. To my immense relief the management in Macau told me that they had full confidence in me and were returning the contract. Perhaps the whole ordeal had been a bit of a test.

One unfortunate effect of only now receiving my full-time contract was that I had to sort out my accommodation independently long after the rest of the group were already settled. Ironically, it was only because I had told the guy in Belgium that I was worried about having to find an apartment by myself in China that I was now in precisely that predicament. Fortunately, I was not completely alone as there was another artist who was new to the show and who also needed somewhere to stay. We house hunted together, and I ended up sharing with her and her husband as well as another flatmate who later moved into the spare room.

I really enjoyed settling into life in Macau. The apartment was in a neighbourhood of high-rise buildings, where virtually everyone was Chinese. I had my go-to places, including a local juice bar and the Blissful Carrot vegetarian restaurant. I enjoyed browsing the Chinese stores and experienced some of the local culture.

I would often walk, run or cycle through the wonderful gardens, occasionally stopping off at a dog-grooming shop where I would look in just to say hello to some furry friends. One day, the shop owner pointed to this little puppy in a cage and said, "You buy?" I took her out of her cage to play with her and give her some water, as her bowl was outside of the cage. She was so cute, and I instantly fell in love. It broke my heart returning her to the cage, and from then on I visited her often. A little while later, I found out that the shop was closing down, and the owner was having to get rid of all the dogs. If I didn't take her, I think she would have been sold to a restaurant. I couldn't live with that guilt, so I agreed to take her.

It wasn't all plain sailing as a dog owner in Macau. On one occasion, I was walking Bella home when four stray street dogs came out of nowhere and tried to attack her. I quickly picked her up but, in doing so, got bitten by one of the dogs and ended up having to have a series of rabies injections, which were very unpleasant.

Besides that awful incident, it was wonderful having a little dog to share my Macau adventures with. I had also completed my training and probation period by now, so was fully settled in, both personally and professionally. I was finally living the dream and life couldn't have been better.

The House of Dancing Water, stingers harness act

The House of Dancing Water, boat act

Russian swing on The House of Dancing Water

7

"F-E-A-R has two meanings: 'Forget Everything And Run' or 'Face Everything And Rise'. The choice is yours."

Zig Ziglar

I knew something was wrong when I spun back into position, but I couldn't quite piece together what had happened, so I carried on and finished the act. One of the technicians unclipped me from my harness and, apparently, I just said, "I'm thirsty," and wandered off. I clearly wasn't feeling myself as, normally, I would always thank the technicians for their hard work, as they keep us performers safe.

In the changing area, I felt really odd and asked the girl next to me if I was bleeding. After that, I crashed out and don't remember much of being rushed to the local hospital.

> **LIFE LESSON #7:** If you ever get injured and need to go to hospital, try not to do it in Macau.

I had sliced open my ear and elbow and now had to have them both stitched back together, using the 'Chinese method', i.e. no anaesthetic. Funnily enough, my elbow was fine – it was so swollen up already that when they stitched it, I didn't feel a thing. My ear, on the other hand… Oh, boy! I don't usually yell out, but on that occasion I unleashed a truly primal scream. My body went into shock and I started sweating hot and cold. The doctor would force a stitch in and then push me into the corner and wait for me to calm down enough for him to do the next one. It was honestly one of the most excruciating experiences of my life.

Once it was all over and I'd had time to recover, I could see that the doctor had actually done a pretty decent job (although some anaesthetic would have been nice!). The scars are now part of my story and a part of me. The one on my elbow is a small blob that I refer to as 'my little slug'. What I didn't know at the time was that the scar on my ear was a distraction from the large swelling just behind it that I paid no attention to. I didn't realise, or even consider, that I had sustained a concussion.

> **LIFE LESSON #8: Our scars tell our stories.**

As it turned out, I had nearly a month off work after that. I couldn't go back into the show while I still had my stitches insitu, I couldn't get them wet. Once they were ready to come out, I was due to fly back home for my annual two-week holiday. We received a fortnight of annual leave, along with two separate one-week breaks, which I would usually use to see more of Southeast Asia. This time I went home and was fine. Or at least, that's what I thought.

Returning to Macau, I was really excited about getting back into the show, but found after only one training session I began to feel unwell. I came over dizzy and thought I was going to be sick. I saw a physio and was sent for tests which confirmed that I had concussion.

Concussion is a serious injury. It takes forever to heal and, in the meantime, you can't do anything that will overstimulate the brain. I had been fully integrated into the show for merely two weeks when the accident happened, and it took me three months to get reintegrated.

A year went by before I encountered my next major hurdle. I had just begun to get my mojo back when I was called into the office again, this time to be told that I needed to lose weight. To be honest, I'd rather not even talk about this period of my life, as it makes me so angry, but I am a firm believer in body positivity, and I do not want to let such a negative episode go unchallenged.

I was 19 years old and being forced to write down everything I ate. I also had to sign up for physio sessions where they would take me to the gym and make me work out. I was scheduled into all the group conditioning sessions and had to do a weigh-in once a week, where I'd print out the piece of paper and then hand it in. I was told that if I didn't reach the target weight they desired within the next six months, they wouldn't renew my contract. I think they saw it as an 'incentive'. I'm not even sure it was legal.

It's worth emphasising that none of this was related to my performances. Nobody was suggesting that my standards were slipping or that I wasn't doing the job properly. It was all just to do with aesthetics and the management's idea of what the 'perfect' weight should be. When I talked about it with my porters (the guys who actually had to lift me) they were extremely supportive, and even joked that lifting a bit more weight only helped make them stronger. Still, I did feel for them in that role – especially since our elaborate costumes added another 2.5kg to the load!

I cannot stress enough how important it is to love the skin that you are in and be proud of who you are. You cannot compare yourself to others as we are all different and come in all shapes and sizes. We could eat the exact same foods, do the exact same workouts and still look completely different.

> **LIFE LESSON #9: Love yourself. You only live once. Enjoy it.**

In the end, I did shed the extra weight, but it had nothing to do with eating less or working out (even) more. It turned out that I had a hormone imbalance and, once that was sorted, I quickly returned to my former weight. Sadly I continued to associate weight gain with what I ate and how hard I trained. It continues to infuriate me how much the directors and physio team were fixated with having me reach a certain number, rather than helping me work out what was going on within my body. They only cared about the aesthetic, which is so wrong. I would honestly hate to be a dancer, as I've heard they have it much worse!

Reflecting back on it now, Macau was intense. And it didn't stop once I'd dealt with the weight issue.

I was working at that stage with a partner on the chandelier, who had come from sports acrobatics and specialised in 'hand-to-hand', a highly demanding trick that involves one acrobat doing a handstand on the outstretched palms of their partner. The angle of the chandelier made this even harder and if it went wrong, the consequences were pretty unpleasant, as it's not much fun falling into the water from five metres at an uncontrolled angle while wearing a heavy costume.

My porter had his contract coming up for renewal and he too was threatened with losing it if we didn't manage to pull off the trick in the show. It felt like blackmail. There were plenty of other couples who were not doing handstands and none of them were being treated like we were. We were also doing things on the chandelier that the others weren't. There was a release trick that we pulled off consistently with no rotation (meaning we would do the act every day, rather than taking turns with the other performers). We were super consistent at that. But none of that seemed to matter to the management. We needed to nail this one particular hand-to-hand trick, or we were out.

It puts a lot of pressure on a working relationship when there are two of you working as a single act – each entirely dependent upon the other. When we practiced the trick on mats in the rehearsal room, I was good. But when we trained above the water, I found the training lights distracting, something about the way they bounced off the water. The days I was trying and trying, but never getting it right, my porter wouldn't speak to me. It was the pressure we were under, and he'd soon let it go, but it would eat away at me inside.

In the end, we decided to start going for it during actual shows. I found it easier in the performances than I did in training, probably because the lighting was less bright during the show. I didn't really feel ready, but the clock was ticking, so we needed to get the trick in. We did it, and my partner kept his contract. In fact, he continued working for the company until the show closed in 2020.

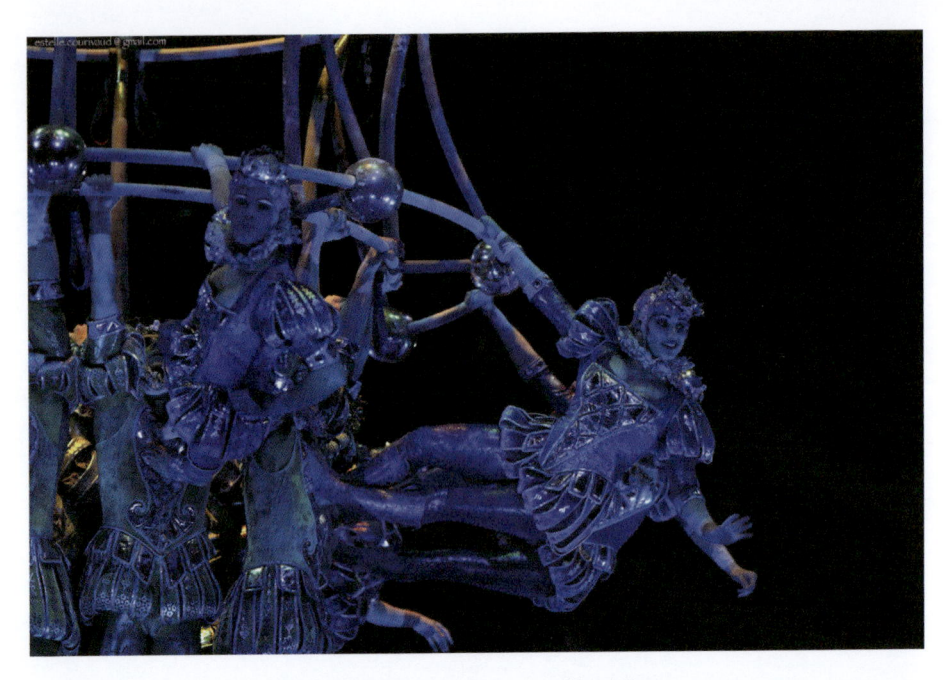

The house of dancing water - Chandelier

Russian swing bow, the House of Dancing Water

8

"Yesterday I was clever, so I wanted to change the world. Today I am wise, so I have begun to change myself."

Rumi

After all the drama that my porter and I had faced in finally getting to grips with our handstands, there was a shuffle within the chandelier group, and we all ended up getting new partners. In the beginning I thought that my new partner Liam didn't like me. However, he soon warmed up when he found how hard I worked. I still do.

We began being more adventurous and creative in our training, just playing around and trying new stuff. Liam helped me master the 'hand-to-hand' and we raised our skill level right across the chandelier act. It was at about that time that we also began to train on the trapeze. Neither of us could later recall what made us try that, although I had always been keen on trying out trapeze tricks.

At this point in my career, I felt that I was ready to move on and experience different avenues of performance. I had wanted to take on a dancing role in the show, for example, but I was too short for the part (aesthetics again!). I did, however, get to be the 'baby swan', which was one of the house troupe roles in the swan dance. That was as good as it was going to get for me in terms of dance, but it did stir up my old passion for artistic performance and stoked the idea of perhaps one day securing the role of a specific character in a show.

In the very first chapter of this book, I talked about having passion for what you are doing and how, should that spark die out, it is time to move on. I had already experienced this as a child with my gymnastics classes, and now I was feeling it again as a young adult. I wanted to perform and grow as an artist and felt that my time in Macau was coming to an end. During my time there, I grew emotionally, accomplished a lot physically and learned life skills. Now I was ready to embrace a new challenge.

When the time came to renew my contract, I decided against signing for another year, as I wanted to investigate other options. I was falling into the unknown and had no idea of what the future had in store. I began thinking about possible back-up careers, should I not find another performing job directly. In the interim I found a course to become a certified personal trainer, which was something that had constantly been of interest. I completed that in my spare time, figuring that, if necessary, I could always head back home as a trainer until I found another circus position. I even got to teach a few classes with members of the show before I left.

Part of the thought process while training on trapeze was that Liam and I could apply for jobs together. Liam and I developed a duo trapeze act which we believed could possibly secure us an employment possibility together, and submitted it by sending a video recording to Cirque du Soleil.

It half worked.

Cirque were looking for a porter to work on a new show that they were creating, but unfortunately the rest of the casting had already been completed and there was no role for me. Liam was undecided because of our commitment, but I persuaded him to accept the position. We had never made any agreements saying that we would stick together no matter what. Plus, he was older than I was, and this was likely his last chance to fulfil his dream of working on a creation with Cirque. I told him to go for it.

A little while later, I was at a barbecue (why do so many key moments in my life occur at barbecues?!) when I received an email from one of the Cirque casting agents. He asked me to call him on Skype, where he explained that a position had come up for a role in their new production, *Luzia*. To make it even more exciting, it was a main character role. Part of the job would also include working as a flyer on a Russian swing act, flying swing to swing – 'the thing' that I had said I would *never* do. So of course, I said yes!

> **LIFE LESSON #10: Never say never**

There were five other women auditioning for the role and I had to send a video presenting myself and my swing skills. The following day at training I threw all the tricks I could think of, including some that I had never done before. I also had to send in a video of me singing, which is something I don't do – or at least something I don't do well. I think they wanted to test my ability to perform and see how well I did when asked to do something outside of my comfort zone, and singing certainly ticked that box. The worst part about the video is that I sang far too close to the camera.

An anxious week dragged by until, finally, I received the good news that I was being offered the position. Yay! Later on, when I finally met the creative team, they mentioned having seen something in my eyes – something that told them I saw the world differently. The show's director, Daniele Finzi Pasca, is honestly one of the most down-to-earth, grounded and humble human beings that I have met.

When he speaks to you, it is as though he sees through you. I feel he emotionally moves people. He recently came to see the show after many years and gave a speech afterwards. It was like hearing the words of a poet and just thinking about it now is enough to bring me to tears. What a very special person.

The circus world is a very supportive community and the people who work in it generally want the best for one another. When I announced the news that I was leaving, my colleagues all wished me well. Well, almost everybody. My head coach on the show was the exception, telling me with a sneer that, "We'll see you back here in six months – you won't last long at Cirque du Soleil." Of course, for someone like me, being told that I won't achieve something just gives me more motivation to prove my doubters wrong.

> **LIFE LESSON #11: Do not dwell on other people's negativity**

Those 'six months' at Cirque du Soleil would, in fact, turn into six fantastic years. I really should send my old head coach an email thanking him for those 'inspirational' parting words!

I had no time to worry about what other people might think, as my life was suddenly very busy. I performed my final show in Franco Dragone, flew home and had two weeks to get my things in order (including rehousing my beloved Chinese dog, Bella, with my ever-so-supportive parents!) before getting ready to move to Montreal, Canada, the home of Cirque du Soleil.

Estelle Courivaud - Photography

The House of Dancing Water bow

Duo Trapeze

The House of Dancing Water, dancer role as a swan

9

"To reach new heights, you have to push yourself. You have to do the work. And you have to test your limits."

Alex Honnold, *Free Solo*

I was totally fired up on the flight to Montreal heading to the home city of Cirque, the company that had first ignited my passion to be a performer. And now I had the privilege of working for them in the creation of a new show.

I arrived at the Cirque residence, which was directly opposite the company's ginormous headquarters. The residence was a quirky box-shaped building and I was soon shown to my 'room', which was, in fact, a studio with a single bed, tiny kitchenette and an en-suite shower. Downstairs, there was a games room, lounge, dining room and a larger kitchen with stoves and ovens. They also had a gym, which included a hot tub. We were fortunate to have someone clean our little apartments once every two weeks. Downstairs there were washing machines and dryers, although sometimes it was a fight to secure one! Unlike when travelling on the road, here we had to take care of our own food and cooking.

On the table was a welcome package explaining everything that would be happening on my first day. I read it over and over, and learned every detail before even unpacking my bags. It wasn't only the jet lag that stopped me from sleeping properly that night. I was about to walk into the headquarters of Cirque du Soleil.

The following day, I crossed the road and walked into the building. It looked like a colossal warehouse that extended three or even more blocks down the road. It was divided into different sections including some *huge* training facilities. I was completely overwhelmed.

Cirque's global headquarters is the base where all the shows around the world are managed, including new shows, production and creation. As well as the training facilities, there are different areas for offices, creative studios, the physio section and physio rooms, production design, rigging, and catering. There were also the four huge studios (which were named A, B, C and P). These came in two different types: one type where they would set up the stage for our particular show, so that we could practise and rehearse; and a second type that was a training facility with all the circus equipment you could dream of.

This would be my home for the next few months, the place where we would take *Luzia* from concept to reality. My first glimpse of the concept was on the designers' mood boards, and it was our job as artists to bring it to life – along with all the various people responsible for the sets, costumes, routines, automation and lighting.

The following three months of creation were as exhilarating as they were exhausting. Being part of a show as it is being assembled – from the artistic director's initial vision to the first night – is such an incredible experience, it sure takes it out of you! I would train before work, followed by conditioning and more training at work. If I ever had a break, I would desperately try to take a nap.

Luzia has a colourful and strong Mexican theme and my character, Running Woman, was inspired by the Tarahumara indigenous tribe who are renowned for their long-distance running prowess. The show is infused with spellbinding magical realism, so much so that my costume also included elements based on the monarch butterflies that migrate every year from Canada to Mexico and back again. For part of the show, I had to run on a treadmill with silk wings trailing behind me – each of them nearly 20 feet long.

The Cirque du Soleil headquarters has the most astonishing fabric, costume, wig, shoe, headdress and mask departments, which make all of the company's prints and costumes. The costumes are even matched with the artist's individual skin tone under special stage lights to give the audience the illusion that there is nothing holding up their costume. Everything is measured and customised to each artist; I had my head scanned in order for the head sections of the costume to be precise, including a sizeable wig that would fit snuggly.

We had a professional make up designer to design each individual character's make up. Once designed, we each had a number of makeup tutorials until we perfected it on ourselves.

At the end of the treadmill sequence, the wings detach from my costume and I act as a tour guide for the other main character, who is looking for water after falling from the sky. Luckily, I have the ethereal ability to summon the rain – with a little bit of help from a highly sophisticated computer-programmed array of water valves that could make beautiful water art and shapes within the shower curtain. This presented a special challenge to the wardrobe department, as all of the shoes and costumes had to be adapted for the water, something that had never been done before. Water was a huge feature in the show, hence the name 'Luzia', which is a fusion of the Spanish words for light (*luz*) and water (*lluvia*).

I'm sure you'll have heard performers talking about 'getting into character' but I found this to be particularly true when it came to the Running Woman. As an emblem of strength and a representative of female empowerment, she was, to me, an embodiment of what I had been striving for in both my personal and professional life. It was a role that helped me overcome fears and take (literal) leaps of faith. It made me contemplate the metamorphosis of life and the power of hope. The character did not define me as a person and I never mistook the Running Woman for Shelli or vice versa, but I did want to keep her power and strength as a permanent part of my own personality.

Oh boy, did I need to be strong in those first few months of creation.

The physical aspect that I just mentioned was one side of it, but there was also the mental strength required to perform safely and successfully on the Russian swing. I had first seen the swing-to-swing version done on *Varekai*, another Cirque show, and that was the time I swore I would *never* do that. The swing act in *The House of Dancing Water* had been demanding enough, and that had involved a much smaller swing, from which we would fly into the water. But for *Luzia*, we had these two gigantic pendulums with a pusher and a catcher stationed on either end to help time the take-off and to support our landings. As one of the flyers, I had to launch myself from the front of the swing and then use my legs to land on the opposite swing. If we missed, there were mats, but no nets to break the fall.

I was once interviewed by a magazine journalist who had previewed the show. He asked whether I ever suffered from nerves and I replied, "Most definitely." And it's true. As a performer, especially on the Russian swing, nerves are what drive you and they are also there for your safety. If you're not nervous about something as challenging as the swing, then you probably shouldn't be jumping!

> **LIFE LESSON #12: A challenge is *meant* to make you nervous. If it doesn't, it probably isn't a challenge.**

As well as being tough physically and tough mentally, that time of my life was tough socially. That might sound strange when you're in this fantastic, creative world, surrounded by a huge bunch of people who share your passion for the circus, but I was in a bit of a strange position with my particular role in the show that left me quite isolated.

The Running Woman character was a solo act. I would interact with other characters in the actual show but for the physical aspects, I was on my own, and this meant that I also rehearsed alone for that part of the show. The Russian swing was all about teamwork but, as the name suggests, it is an act that traditionally involves Eastern European artists. I was working with Russians, Belarusians and Ukrainians, and I was the only English person. There was one girl on the team who was Ukrainian but spoke English fluently, so she helped me to communicate with the others, and ended up becoming back-up for my role as well as a really good friend. I was given Russian lessons but, just as with my 'taxi language Cantonese', I didn't get far – basically just the main terminology for the swing. In the end, their English was always going to be better than my Russian.

It was a somewhat lonely period despite being surrounded by people. I was fortunate to connect with an old friend. She kindly 'adopted' me during my stay in the city, and it was so nice to have some comfort and a home away from home.

Finally, all the training came to an end and it was time for the opening night in Montreal. Expectations were high, especially as there would be a load of press invited to the premiere. I remember arriving at the big top and being able to feel the excitement in the air, mixed in with the heady scent of popcorn!

Before each show, we do a group warm-up to get us into 'the zone'. Everybody wishes one another 'merde' (the circus equivalent of 'break a leg'). Once the warm-up is over, I finish my final 'touch ups' before heading backstage. I'm always early and eager; the last thing I'd want is to be late.

It is dark backstage, but I have my two wingmen with me. And by 'wingmen' I literally mean the performers who are attached to my belt with the giant butterfly wings and who are responsible for the wings' movement and eventual removal. I wish them a good show. In my zone, I block everything out. Fittingly, I have butterflies in my stomach. I glance down at the floor, visualising all the rehearsals. I glance up, determination gleaming through my eyes. I'm ready to run. The music begins, my cue goes, the curtains open. Its time. *Allez*! Let's do this, let's go!

Afterwards, I run off stage, feeling such a rush. It's hard to gauge if the audience enjoyed it or not! So much was going through my head that I could barely remember the applause. There is little time to reflect in any case, as this was only the beginning. My character is in the opening scene but there was a whole show to get through, including my big finish on the Russian swing!

Backstage, there is a live stream of the show on a TV, which we all crowd around to watch and support one another. As soon as one act comes off backstage there is a line-up of people waiting to celebrate and give congratulations and high fives. It is, honestly, the most supportive environment. Everyone just wants the best for one another.

During the intermission my nerves start to build up as I begin preparing myself for the swing. I make sure I have a really good warm up backstage and then go through the tunnel to get back into the zone with the help of my pre-performance rituals.

Deep breaths.

Shaking off my nerves, it is time to fly high.

I try not to think too much and just do it. So I did, and

it was perfect. After my jump, my adrenaline spiked and I could relax and enjoy the rest of the performance. I knew this was going to be the new normal and I would have to get used to that every single night and for 10 shows a week.

As the opening night came to a close, we took our bows and heard the roar of the audience. We had done it – the first show of many successfully in the bag. To think, this was one of the thousands that we would do over the next six years, but it's always the first that you will never forget.

After the show, we had a massive celebration backstage and quickly removed our makeup, which comes off in five seconds as opposed to the 30-45 minutes it takes to apply! We then got changed and ready to join everyone at the front of house to celebrate.

I was still smiling the next day as I read the opening night reviews. One critic described the show as "an explosion of joy that proves [Cirque du Soleil] still have what it takes to create a profoundly touching, finger-on-the-pulse spectacle". The Montreal Gazette wrote that:

"Luzia was an absolute pleasure to watch – not just for the high-octane tricks but as a spectacular and cohesive theatrical experience that was successful on every level. If you've skipped seeing the Cirque for a few years, this is truly a show to bring you back into the fold. Bravo."

And, as one of the iconic characters who got to open the show, I also came in for some positive reviews, including one that said that, "Shelli Epstein, as the emblematic Running Woman, was superb – strong, beautiful and in possession of buckets of stage presence."

Not bad for the former child gymnast who was once so shy of the spotlight!

Luzia, Running Woman

Luzia, Running Woman

Luzia, Running Woman with the horse puppet

10

"You have brains in your head. You have feet in your shoes. You can steer yourself any direction you choose."
Dr. Seuss, *Oh, the Places You'll Go!*

When I first fell in love with the circus, it was all about the sublime surrealism of what I saw on stage – the combination of breathtaking colours, costumes, artistry and the emotion, physical strength and grace of the performers.

I already touched on a little about the incredible, meticulous work of the technicians behind the scenes in Macau. In Montreal, I witnessed close-up the wonder of a show being created – from the artists' vision boards to the opening night. Finally, after nine months in Montreal, as the big top came down (another technical feat that always boggles my mind), it was time for my first experience of taking that show on the road.

As a touring show, *Luzia* was staged in a purpose-built big top that could seat 2,500 people. The tent incorporated all the necessary facilities for the show, including a training space backstage, a kitchen with chefs who would provide meals for us, a gym, showers, and areas for the physios to treat us. There were showers and special washing machines used for our costumes as well as regular washing machines for artists to do their personal laundry. Outside the big tent, there were prefabricated offices whose occupants were responsible for the logistics of the show.

Every time we moved cities, all of this paraphernalia had to be taken down and packed onto containers, transported and then set up in the following city. It was a massive undertaking, and we would all have to chip in.

We were a large group of performers, from jugglers, contortionists and strong men to hoop divers, tumblers and Russian swing artists, not to mention all the musicians. And then there were all the people involved in the lighting, special effects, carpentry, sound, automation, wardrobe and stage management. There were the directors, the coaches, the accountants, the tent masters, the site guys which included security. In total, we were 45 performers supported by 80 additional specialists.

The stage management team are *the* most organised people you will ever meet. They are in charge of scheduling and time management as well as having the responsibility to call the show. I already mentioned this in regard to *The House of Dancing Water,* where it was on an even larger scale. It is an enormous responsibility to ensure that a show like *Luzia* runs smoothly and efficiently, so that, if things go wrong, the audience are none the wiser. An example of this was when we had a technical error with the treadmills not working and I had to run on a stationary belt. Another time one of the winches used by an aerialist got stuck. The show must go on!

Another aspect of life on tour was the shock and surprise of seeing my face all over the new city, be it on billboards, buses or trains – or even Times Square in New York. My character Running Woman had become the face of the show. I never quite got used to that, but it did make me smile. My character was made into a doll that was sold at the front of house, including butterfly wings. It was really cute seeing children leaving the tent with their wings.

Had I not joined the circus at 18, by this point in my life I would have been leaving university and looking for my first job. How much I would have missed out on had I just carried on going down the expected path.

I have been so fortunate to travel extensively and enjoy the rich experience that arises from living in a foreign country. Macau had provided me with a base from which to explore parts of Asia. *The House of Dancing Water* was open five days a week, which meant I was able to use my two days off to make short trips to other parts of mainland China and Hong Kong. I also took full advantage of the week-long holidays we were given. I visited Japan – and was struck by how vastly different it was to China. Cambodia and Vietnam were beautiful but also highly emotional with such tragic, intertwined histories. The Maldives was pure bliss. I took advantage of my time there and I completed my open water scuba training, which I then put to good use in Australia, exploring the Great Barrier Reef and swimming with barracuda (which are far scarier than sharks in my opinion!). I also squeezed in Singapore, Myanmar, the Philippines and Thailand during those three years in Macau.

> **LIFE LESSON #13:** Nothing changes your perspective on life as much as travel. Whenever you have the chance to go somewhere new, take it.

I loved my 10 months spent in Montreal, from creation to completing our final performance. It remains one of my favourite cities and has so much to offer. Montreal is the place where circus is truly appreciated as an artform since it is the home of Cirque du Soleil.

Many of the performers and technicians are based in Montreal, making for a big social scene and *a lot* of partying. The company parties were legendary. I remember the Christmas party in particular, where they had a drag queen DJ, karaoke, an inflatable surfboard ride, a barber to cut the guys' hair and a nail bar for the women, and all these amazing food platters and drinks bars – including cocktails that you drank from chocolate cups. There was also an insane summer party to mark Cirque's 35th anniversary, for which they set up full-on roller coasters. The one thing I was pleased not to endure a second time was the Montreal winter! It was pretty grim! I remember when they put the big top up, it was minus 40 degrees! Of course, there are all sorts of activities like skiing that become available during the winter months, but we were contractually prevented from participating to avoid injury, so it was really just a case of hunkering down and waiting for spring to arrive.

After Montreal, the tour kicked off with the relatively short hop over to Toronto, which is another really fun city. I lived in the heart of downtown for three months and was able to show off like a local when my sister and then, later, my grandparents visited to see the show and visit Niagara Falls.

San Francisco was next on the list for a three-month stay. This would be my first time in the US, and I was really looking forward to the experience. In many ways it was a great introduction to the country, seeing the iconic Golden Gate Bridge, the Walt Disney Museum and enjoying all the parks and nature – but also getting glimpses of the dark underbelly, with so much homelessness. The artists experienced theft – people's bikes being stolen left, right and centre.

In San Francisco, we experienced the absolute worst moment of the tour, when one of the technicians suffered a fatal accident backstage. There are obviously dangerous elements to the circus, so health and safety is absolutely paramount in everything we do. Tragically, something went wrong that day, and a piece of heavy equipment fell on him. I was backstage at the time and heard the crash. We were then told to go to our dressing rooms so that the emergency services could have clear access.

It was a devastating time for all of us, and the show went dark (no performances) for a week. The company provided psychologists and gave us all the support we needed. I was in absolute shock, as were my fellow artists. We experienced this tragedy together and bonded over it too, making us into a cohesive *Luzia* family. Unanimously, we decided to reopen and dedicate the first show back to our colleague. The big top was renamed in his memory and every year we would dedicate a show to him.

Cirque du Soleil provides its artists with top notch accommodation at each of the show locations – usually a serviced apartment shared with another employee. San Jose, our next stop, was the first place where I turned down the company's accommodation offer and rented a place with three other people from the show. That was a really nice time as we were near to a high street and some local gyms.

It's quite a chill city and I found it to be a bit strange. The downtown area, in particular, was like something from a zombie apocalypse movie, with very few people about and the shops always seeming to be closed at weird times.

We moved on to Seattle where I plucked up the courage to rent a car, having never driven an automatic or on the 'wrong' side of the road before. This enabled me to explore not just the hyper-cool city itself but also the beautiful natural surroundings. It reminded me of the UK a little, especially in terms of the climate.

Summertime came around as we approached the end of the first year on tour, and I loved spending time in Denver. It has a nice small-city feel to it and it was great to feel the sun on my skin. The Montreal winter felt like a lifetime ago! At first glance, it's easy to think that North America is pretty much the same wherever you go… however, it is this vast expanse of land, people and culture. Spending time there, I was able to immerse myself in the different local cultures, as well as happily ticking off all the touristy things that each city had to offer. I really enjoyed getting to understand the different customs and mentalities of the various states and regions.

When we arrived in Chicago, I remember thinking how life could not get much better. Our big top was set up next to the Chicago Bulls stadium, where we had the opportunity to check out their facilities. I was loving the variety of visiting all these new places and staying just long enough to get to know them without ever getting bored. The show had received fantastic reviews and we were all starting to feel comfortable without ever getting complacent – as I continued to hone my skills on the Russian swing.

Everyone knows the saying, that 'what goes up must come down,' and it's certainly a concept that you learn early as an acrobat. And so it was in Chicago, when everything was going so well, that I found myself facing my next big challenge.

Surfing in Hawaii

Washington DC

Australia

Diving with whale sharks in the Philippines

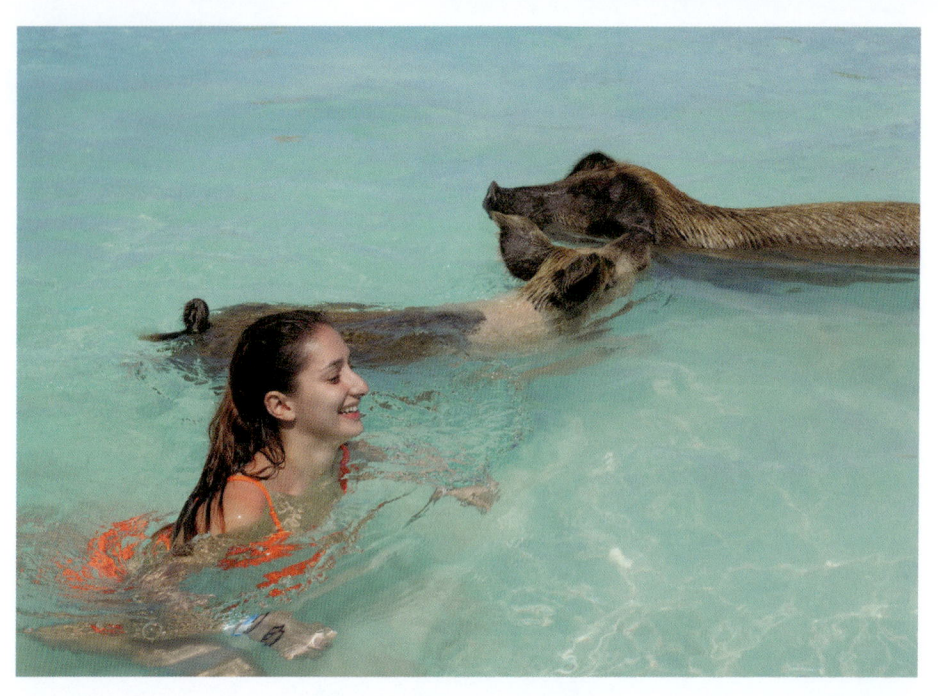

Swimming with pigs in the Bahamas

Silver back gorilla in Rwanda

Banff, Lake Louise, Alberta Canada while the show was in Calgary

11

"There is no passion to be found playing small – in settling for a life that is less than the one you are capable of living."
                                                            Nelson Mandela

I cannot emphasise enough how important it is to listen to one's body, and not to ignore it when it is sending clear signals to slow down. Yet as a professional athlete and performer who makes a living from pushing the limits of her body on a daily basis, I also know how difficult it is to follow that advice.

Prior to arriving in Chicago I had felt some pain in my right ankle. I had ignored it and pushed on. Any high-level athlete might take a painkiller to make it through the next match or tournament – rather than accepting that they need to rest up.

I hadn't made a secret of the fact that I was hurting, and had even been told not to do any additional training outside of the scheduled work sessions. I ignored that. After 12 weeks of the pain not clearing, it was company policy that I see a doctor. He requested an MRI scan, but I honestly didn't think it was going to come back as anything other than normal inflammation (or what passes for 'normal' in the circus world).

The scan came back with...

Stress reaction (talus bone)

Spring ligament strain

Posterior tibial tendonitis

Plantar fasciitis

So definitely not normal. I was put into a boot for the first time in my life and was so upset that I started crying. I was instructed to stop performing and continue with physiotherapy. I managed to partake in my regular Orange Theory and Barry's fitness classes, while still wearing the boot, only working on the upper body elements.

Cirque were really supportive. Since I was unable to perform, they even gave me some time off to join my family for a week.

When the show moved on to Atlanta, I was mainly in 'cues' – which is when you are back on the stage, but not doing any of the main parts. I had to build up enough ankle strength to start doing the Running Woman sections and was only allowed to practise swing using a harness, which helped minimise the pressure of the landings. By the end of 2017, around six months after the initial MRI scan, I was finally able to reintegrate into the full show in Los Angeles.

It had been a tough old time and required patience and moderation – not always my strongest suits – but at least I had been able to stay on tour with the company and have the support of friends and colleagues who had a good idea of what I was dealing with. I would later find out how much harder it is when you have to do all that on your own.

Our next city was Los Angeles. One day, returning from my usual morning class, I found police outside my apartment block. I didn't think much of it and went up to my room to shower before going to rehearse a dance piece outside on the common floor, which had an open grass area. At this point, a policeman approached us and told us we had to return to our rooms as there were police snipers on the roofs of other buildings looking for a suspect with a gun!

Not being from America, the whole gun thing was very foreign to me – and still is. The building was in lockdown and we were told not to leave. Eventually, we were released and could get onto the bus for work, eager to find out what had happened. This was definitely a Hollywood movie moment living in La La Land.

My ankle stayed intact for another year and a half and I threw myself back into life on tour, feeling even more grateful for the amazing opportunities. We hopped from one side of the country to the next when we left LA for

Washington D.C. My parents were supposed to come meet me in Washington D.C., but cancelled their trip when my father crashed a quadbike in the sand dunes of South Africa and ended up in hospital with a fractured pelvis and dislocated hip. It seems injury is a family trait!

Our 'Washington' accommodation was situated in Virginia, next to a shopping mall. It was pretty far out, so weekends were saved for exploring. On the weekends, I would head into the capitol and soak up all the amazing history, monuments and museums. After Washington, we headed north to Boston, another fabulous city steeped in history

Then came Mexico, definitive highlight of the tour. I would recommend Mexico to anyone. Performing a Mexico-themed show in front of Mexicans was such an honour. It felt strange to be walking around and seeing all these sights and images that I recognised from the show: the hearts, the masked 'luchador' wrestlers, *papel picado*, *cenotes*, coyotes, butterflies and hummingbirds – all out there in real life. I kept spotting stuff and thinking that they'd taken it from *Luzia* and had to keep reminding myself that *no, the creators of* Luzia *have taken that from Mexico!*

The most moving experience for me personally was getting to see the monarch butterflies whose migration from Canada to Mexico provided some of the inspiration for the show and influenced the design of my Running Woman costume. We were taken to see the sites where the butterflies cluster together upside down in huge groups over winter. There are so many of them spread out over the trees that, at first, you think they are thorns. Many of them can also be seen dead on the ground. It takes three to four generations to make the 6,000-mile round trip journey from Canada, meaning that no individual butterfly ever comes close to completing the whole trip

> **LIFE LESSON #14:** Let nature inspire you. There is so much that humans can learn from our fellow inhabitants on this earth.

I have no words to describe the anxiety I felt ahead of the Luzia premier in Mexico. The crowd was eerily silent and I was worried that it wasn't going well. Fortunately, it turned out that they were in awe at seeing the way in which Cirque du Soleil had taken all these elements of their homeland and turned them into such a beautiful and reverential homage to the country. The cheers we received at the end of the Mexican shows were the loudest I have ever heard.

Whilst in Mexico we toured Guadalajara, Monterrey, and Mexico City. Between cities, I did my own travel to Mérida and the surrounding state of Yucatán, as well as the Cancún area. One of my favourite highlights was diving with whale sharks and manta rays!

Leaving the vibrancy of Mexico for the theme park artificiality of Orlando probably felt like a bit of a comedown for most of the cast and crew, not for me, I'm a massive Disney fan so I loved it. I even participated in the Disney half marathon, having to start at five in the morning because of the heat. My ankle was quite sore thereafter, so I guess I overdid it a little, but it was worth it for the thrill of running past all the iconic Disney locations. The only major disappointment in Orlando was that the show didn't do as well as it had in the other locations. The problem suspected was there had previously been a resident Cirque du Soleil show, and people had assumed that it was the same show and they thought that they had already seen it.

Ticket sales were soon the last thing on my mind, as we moved on to New York and I injured myself again – this time in the middle of the show and far more seriously.

It happened while I was doing a dismount (jumping from the swing to the fly mat). My ankle buckled as I landed. I felt and heard my ankle pop from underneath me. I was telling myself *I'm fine, I'm fine*, but as soon as I tried to step off the mat, the pain engulfed me and I welled up with tears. One of the other performers had seen what had happened and he scooped me up and rushed me backstage. After a quick inspection in the tent's medical area, I was sent off to the hospital and, before long, found myself back in a boot – this time with crutches too.

It was all very frustrating but after my experience in

Chicago, I thought I knew what was to come. I would stay on the tour, do some more physiotherapy and then get myself back into the show. It didn't turn out that way. By the time we had moved on to Connecticut I had my first appointment with the physios. It did not mirror the Chicago meeting. The hospital scans had revealed serious ligament damage and it was explained to me that this is worse than a break because it takes much longer to heal and is never quite the same again. Since it was a long-term injury, there was no point me continuing on the tour. They would be sending me home to complete my rehabilitation there.

I remember sitting there, looking down at my ankle on the physio bench, and thinking, *What?*

Monarch butterflies migration in Mexico!

New York City, 2019

12

"And when you're in a Slump, you're not in for much fun. Unslumping yourself is not easily done."
Dr. Seuss, Oh, the Places You'll Go!

At Cirque, if an individual gets injured, they are either treated on site or sent home should the injury require an extended rehabilitation. When they realised the extent of my injury, I was sent home to recover.

On the one hand, it was exciting to be heading back home after seven years away, and I would also make it home in time to surprise my sister on her birthday. On the other hand, I knew that the show must go on – but it was going on without me. The first few weeks were particularly difficult as I was confined to my boot and couldn't even exercise.

I worked out the time difference between the UK and the cities where *Luzia* was showing and drove myself crazy thinking about what would be happening on the stage at that precise moment while I was home doing nothing.

It's important to stress that I was not simply abandoned by Cirque. When performers under contract are injured, they are still paid, albeit not at the full rate (I was on about 75% of my pay), and I had also been given a detailed rehabilitation programme. I had become so used to being on tour and performing that I now felt alone, isolated and lost.

There was also the fact that, just like with the show, my family's lives continued as normal. My parents and my sister were working, and my brother was still at school, but I had nowhere to go and no purpose beyond my physiotherapy – and I could only do that for a few hours a week. I also struggled with my loss of independence. After seven years of living on my own and fending for myself in different cities all over the world, I was suddenly stuck at home.

There were two questions that my dad always asked me: "When are you coming home next?" and "What are you going to do with your life after the circus?" For now, the first question was well and truly answered, but I realised that I did need to start thinking seriously about the answer to the second question. Being off the tour and injured, was a real wake-up call that I would eventually have to make some big career decisions. It increased my motivation to return to the show, to avoid facing those dilemmas.

I started to make a routine for myself at home. Finally, I came out of the boot and could increase my physio rehab. I managed to stop dwelling on the negative aspects of being home and started to appreciate the positives. I went out and explored the city and found myself falling in love with it. I managed to see numerous circus shows when they were in town, which increased my appreciation for circus as an art form.

Three months passed by and I was able to run again, which meant I could do the bare minimum required for the Running Woman part of the show. I needed a doctor to sign me off, stating that I was fit enough to return to work. Strangely I found that I was comfortable being back home and was enjoying being in London. As my birthday was approaching, I began wishing I could stay a little longer and celebrate with my family. However, I had received the all clear to return to work and I set out with trepidation, hoping that no more injuries would come my way.

> **LIFE LESSON #15:** Human beings adapt quickly to new circumstances – and not always for the better. If you are in a rut, search out the positives and focus on them fully.

I convinced myself that *yes, I can do it,* and that my experience of being off the tour was only going to increase my drive to excel in the show for as long as I could. I knew there were still questions for me to answer regarding my future plans long term, but that was for another day. For now, I knew exactly where I needed to be.

Russian swing dismount

Luzia, swing to swing

13

"Perhaps the butterfly is proof that you can go through a great deal of darkness yet become something beautiful."

Beau Taplin

I re-joined the tour in Calgary. After my experiences with concussion in Macau and stress fractures in Chicago, this would be my third go at reintegrating into a show. I was simply determined that I would make it.

I had the biggest motivation that you could dream of to regain full fitness levels when it was announced that we would be starting the European leg of the show in London, my home city. The best part was that I would be performing in front of my friends and family in the Royal Albert Hall, the venue where I had first fallen in love with the circus as an 11-year-old girl.

As we reached the end of our stay in Calgary, I was sent

home by the company once again – not on account of injury, this time, but to carry out a load of PR interviews for the London show, mainly to sell the story of 'local girl comes home'. I was invited onto several TV shows, including the BBC's primetime *One Show* and another one where I had to do a little skit with one of the jugglers from *Luzia*. Another promotional event was held at the Royal Geographical Society. I remember one day when I had to do four or five make-up changes! After the London promotions I flew to Vancouver for a three-month stint, where I managed to master all my tricks on the Russian swing and work more tricks into the show.

Everything went perfectly, or as close to perfectly as possible. I still felt pain in my ankle, but this had become my 'new normal' and the ankle itself was holding. Eventually, the pain subsided and I was able to master bigger and more exciting tricks. We were due to premiere in London in January 2020 and I had just enough time after the final show in Vancouver to make it back home for New Year's Eve (though I was so jet lagged that I fell asleep before midnight).

Finally, the time had arrived. To go back to where it all began...

Initially, it felt surreal being in London surrounded by all my friends from the cast and crew of *Luzia*. After the previous years, being a professional tourist, and soaking up the sights and sounds of foreign cities, suddenly I was the one being asked for all the insider tips and must-see places. To be honest, I had been away for so long that I wouldn't have had a clue what to reply, had it not been for my recent injury lay-off when I'd had the chance to reacquaint myself with my home city.

Putting on a show at the Royal Albert Hall is actually tougher than I'd imagined, especially in January when the British weather is not exactly at its best. The cast were used to performing in the tent, where there is a constant source of fresh air circulating, whereas in the hall, albeit a magnificent, old and historic building, there was lots of dust and the ventilation was poor. Our training area was situated upstairs and had no windows. A lot of artists started coming down with colds and flu-like symptoms. There was also talk about a deadly new virus that was circulating in China and threatening to spread to Europe, although most of us were too busy with rehearsing to pay much attention to that…

On the first days of rehearsals I walked around the Royal Albert Hall, looking at the photos on the foyer walls of the various famous actors and artists who had once performed there. Stepping out into the hall itself and seeing those famous red seats, from where I'd watched my first live circus all those years ago. Even during training, as I stepped out from the wings, I couldn't stop myself from looking around, pinching myself. This was for real, I had arrived! To be in this stunning location in my home city, standing on the stage where so many of my idols had stood – it was hard not to be overwhelmed. 'Euphoria' is the word that springs to mind to describe how I felt. I was bursting with pride and joy. The only way I could release it would be by performing.

> **LIFE LESSON #16:** It's important to focus on the road ahead, but it can also be good to glance back in the mirror now and again to see how far you've come.

Given how much emotional investment I had in these London shows, it could easily have turned into an anti-climax but, fortunately, those seven weeks at the Royal Albert Hall were just as magical as I had hoped. While in Vancouver, I had been training to perform a particularly demanding Russian swing trick, happily I had become consistent enough to take the safety lines off during training in London, and managed to premiere the trick on opening night. I have no idea whether the audience appreciated it, but it's a trick that experienced acrobats respect because it involves a blind landing. One takes off from the launch swing but then flips in the air in such a way that you can´t see the landing swing as you approach it. Instead, you have to feel for the swing with your feet and only realise where you are once you've made contact.

I had no pain at all during the London shows – maybe because I was on such a high – and my ankle felt stronger and healthier than it had done in years. I was allowed a few complimentary tickets for family, including my grandparents from Israel and my grandpa from South Africa. Sadly, my wonderful grandmother had passed away three years earlier so she never got to see me in *Luzia*, although there had been a weird moment just before the Russian swing at the show's premiere in Montreal when I could have sworn I heard her voice, so maybe she was there to see me after all.

Before I knew it, it was time for the final show in London, and my mum, dad, brother, sister, and my sister's boyfriend were all there to see it.

I don't understand why I feel way more nervous when there are people I know in the audience. For this final London show, it probably helped calm me down a little that my parents had seen it a few times already. In any case, it all went smoothly and I was able to savour every second of the curtain call. I blew so many kisses out into the crowd and gestured my thank-yous to my family. After all the doubts I'd had as to whether I would ever make it – make it into the professional circus world, make it into Cirque du Soleil, make it back from injuries, make it to the Royal Albert Hall – this was a moment I planned to savour.

I knew it was my last bow in London and so wanted to take it for what it was. I remember wondering if I would ever get another chance to perform the show in my home city. I had no way of knowing that this would possibly be the last time I could perform at all.

Luzia, end of act one, handloop

Luzia, swing to same swing, three jumps

Luzia, Royal Albert Hall

14

"It is strange, but true, that the most important turning-points of life often come at the most unexpected times and in the most unexpected ways.'

Napoleon Hill

I was fortunate to work in some of the world's best circus hot spots, including China, Canada, the United States, London. Now it was time for Russia… I was so excited about visiting another country with a rich circus tradition – not to mention performing on the Russian swing along with my Russian and Eastern European colleagues.

Sadly, our visit lasted for precisely six days.

I can't imagine there will be many memoirs written about the 2020s that don't come to a grinding halt with the sudden appearance of the Covid-19 virus, and my own story is no exception. By the time we performed the final London show on 1st March 2020, the virus that people had started to whisper about during the rehearsals had grown into a full-scale global pandemic. It was actually officially declared as such by the World Health Organisation on 11th March, the very day that we flew out to Moscow.

We had originally been due to fly on 12th March, but Cirque brought our flights forward by a day in an attempt to avoid us all having to go into quarantine upon arrival. Rumour had it that Russia was about to put the UK on its red list of countries from where arriving passengers would have to self-isolate, so it was a real race against time.

We arrived at a near empty airport and walked out into what looked like a ghost town. We had daily meetings to assess the situation, looking at what was happening in Russia and also around the world. People were starting to get anxious as more and more international borders were closed and things became increasingly uncertain. The technicians were particularly concerned, pointing out that the artists had all had 10 days off after the final London show and many had taken the opportunity to travel back to their families or grab a quick vacation. Travel, of course, increased the chances of somebody having picked up the virus and we were now all meant to hunker down together in the Palace of Gymnastics.

We were one of the last shows trying to stay open and it was decided to put the matter to a vote. The majority view was that we could not go ahead and that was that.

The sets were dismantled and everything was boxed away. We managed to have a quick look around the sights – the Kremlin, Red Square – and then, on 16th March, we were all sent home.

To say it was a strange time would be an understatement. The UK seemed a little slower to grasp the seriousness of the situation than other places, and I flew back from the empty streets of Moscow to a London where people were still travelling into work, piling onto trains and attending their regular gym classes. Of course, that changed soon enough, and it wasn't long before we joined most of the world in full-on lockdown.

Like many other people who weren't directly affected by the virus, I tried to focus on the positives. The management at Cirque were confident that the tour would resume, with some changes to the itinerary, within two to three months – starting in the Canary Islands and then moving on to Spain and, in 2021, Japan. They even arranged for our personal belongings to be transported from Moscow to Amsterdam, ready to be shipped to the Canaries. At the time of writing, a lot of my personal belongings are still somewhere in Amsterdam.

So, like everybody else, I threw myself into some new hobbies and made a start on some projects I'd always planned to do if I ever found the time (such as writing my memoirs!) and waited for my call-up back to work.

The call-up never came. Instead, an email was sent out

to the entire cast and crew including a video that Cirque had prepared. We were told to press 'play'. It was all rather corporate (especially for a circus company!) and included lots of HR jargon, but I picked up on a distinction they were making between Vegas-based shows and the rest of us who they were "having to let go". My dad and my brother were with me at the time and, when the video finished, I turned to them and asked, "Did I just get fired?" They both nodded back at me.

It was a hard pill to swallow, and also a sudden reminder of how fleeting careers in the entertainment industry can be (during a global pandemic or otherwise). I felt better prepared, though, than I had during my first forced lay-off, following my ankle injury in New York. For starters, I'd had those first few months when lockdown had still seemed like more of a holiday than an imprisonment.

Looking back on that first period away from the circus, I could see now that it had been a real crisis of identity. I hadn't known who Shelli was, once she was no longer Shelli the circus performer. Ironically, it was recognising that which helped me find my sense of purpose during the global lockdown. I started to think about all the other artists and performers who face similar crises and wondered what was available to help them. I recalled having spoken to a sports psychologist who had spent some time with the cast of *Luzia* and we had talked about the general lack of support for artists beyond what is provided to help them fulfil their roles on stage. I had heard of professional athletes and military personnel being coached in how to transition into the 'real world' at the end of their sporting or army careers, but was unaware of anything similar for artists. That's one of the things I'm thinking about offering. More generally, I'd like to share with people from all walks of life, to help them achieve their goals by using some of the lessons and techniques that I have picked up from my circus career.

So, at the age of 28, having never been to university, I decided to become a student again and enrolled in a sports psychology course. I also decided to utilise the personal training certificate that I received in Macau and applied to every gym in the area. It turned out that lockdown was not the best time to be approaching gyms, which had all been forced to close. Luckily, there was certainly lots of interest in keeping fit. As a result I started offering fitness and running sessions online and slowly built up a client base for one-to-one tuition. Once the lockdown restrictions began to lift, I was called up by one of the gyms that I'd contacted and offered a part-time job teaching group classes – which is my favourite type of class.

If it sounds like an easy switch, from circus performer to performance coach, it wasn't, and it's something I am still working on.

> **LIFE LESSON #17:** Reinventing yourself is hard; trying to do too much too quickly doesn't always work. Slow and steady wins the race.

My commitment to my new path was tested in 2021, when I was offered a potential opportunity to return to the circus. I had finally found something in life that I could contemplate doing post-circus, and it's been good for me to discover who Shelli is without her being defined by that circus world.

I haven't completely ruled out a return ("Never say never," remember!) but, right now, it feels good to keep my options open. I don't know yet what life has in store for me, so I'm flying a little blind and am not quite sure where I'm going to land.

> **LIFE LESSON #18:** Life is like a train journey; every stop where you disembark offers new adventures and possibilities – embrace them.

Luzia, Russian swing cross

Luzia, Running Woman

Luzia, front layout swing to swing

Last day performing at the Royal Albert Hall March 1st 2020

EPILOGUE

"How does one become a butterfly? You must want to fly so much that you are willing to give up being a caterpillar."

Trina Paulus

This is not a story with an ending. At the age of 28, I still have little idea what the future holds, or even what next year holds, so it feels like I'm only coming to the juicy middle part!

At the time of writing, it looks possible that Cirque du Soleil will resume *Luzia* in January 2022, at the Royal Albert Hall. Contracts are being drawn up and, after coming to terms with doing my 'final' show there, it's just about conceivable that I could pick up exactly where I left off.

Whether that happens or not, I honestly believe that circus will forever be a part of me. It's like a version of that old saying: you can take the girl out of the circus, but you can't take the circus out of the girl! Circus has given me so many important skills, both physically and mentally. It has taught me lessons that I still regularly apply to my day-today life. It doesn't totally define me in the way that it once did, but it has certainly helped to make me who I am today.

For now, it feels like the butterfly is cocooned inside of me, waiting for her moment to shine. In fact, I can still hear the beats of my Running Woman routine in my head, and I thought that might make a fitting 'end' to this part of my story. It is simply the running order of things I had to do for the show, from applying my make-up to taking the final bow, but someone once told me that it sounded like a poem. I think, for me, maybe it is.

Luzia, Running Woman

RUNNING WOMAN ROUTINE

Apply make up
Wig prep; leg, stripes and spots
Wig
Arms
Belt

Back stage right
Clip in wings
Key turns
I hear my cue
and am no longer Shelli…

"Running Woman, go!"
I run, jump, bow

Exit stage left
Return belt
Remember to drink water

Enter backstage left
Walk through fields of cacti
Call the rain
Exit stage right

Return stage left with horse
Majo sings
Horse
Spin
Dance with Eric

Backstage left

Intermission

Backstage left
Exit right

Jaguar

Change / warm up

Candles

Swing
Backstage right
My passage backstage in the tunnel
Mental prep
Breathing
Focus

Finish swing
Fiesta

Dancing with Eli
We freeze

Always thinking about how it feels to be on stage
How the lights shine on you
Looking up at the lights
Something I'll never forget

Those precious moments backstage
I miss the stage
I long for one more show
One last time

What else can I say
There's so much
But, at the same time, I have no words.

The sound of the audience reaction
Fills my heart to the brim

It feels so good it hurts.

Shelli Epstein, September 2021

The cross jump on Luzia

Bow on Luzia at the Royal Albert Hall

PHOTO CREDITS

Front cover: Claudia Fernández-Arango (photography), Eme Lanoir (make-up)

Page 47 ,54, 55, 64, 71 and 73: Estelle Courivaud

Page 72: Tom Fairchild

Page 84, 115 and 133: Bircan Tulga, Black Edge Productions

Page 85, 86, 123, 124, 134 ,135, 138, 142, 143: Eglantine Lepetit

Page 96 (top Photo), 98 (top Photo), 108: Nelson Smyles

Page 109: Todd Morgan Kent Jr

Page 99: Abou Traore

Story Terrace

Printed in Great Britain
by Amazon